DISCARD

D1527413

UNSOLVED MYSTERIES

The D. B. Cooper Hijacking

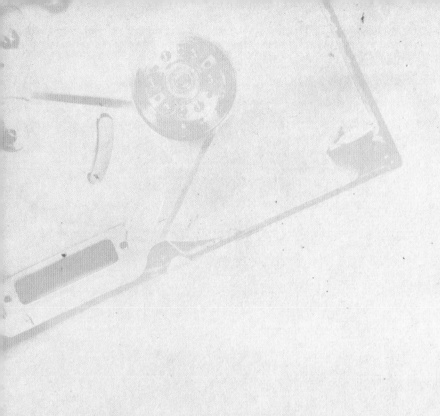

ABDO
Publishing Company

The D. B. Cooper Hijacking

By Marcia Amidon Lusted

Content Consultant
Mike Stapleton
Forensics Consultant
CEO, Stapleton & Associates, LLC

CREDITS

Published by ABDO Publishing Company, PO Box 398166
Minneapolis, MN 55439. Copyright © 2012 by Abdo Consulting
Group, Inc. International copyrights reserved in all countries.
No part of this book may be reproduced in any form without
written permission from the publisher. The Essential Library™ is a
trademark and logo of ABDO Publishing Company.

Printed in the United States of America,
North Mankato, Minnesota
102011
012012

 THIS BOOK CONTAINS AT LEAST 10% RECYCLED MATERIALS.

Editor: Melissa York
Copy Editor: Kathryn-Ann Geis
Series design: Becky Daum, Christa Schneider, & Ellen Schofield
Cover production: Christa Schneider
Interior production: Becky Daum

Library of Congress Cataloging-in-Publication Data
Lusted, Marcia Amidon.
  The D.B. Cooper hijacking / by Marcia Amidon Lusted.
     p. cm. -- (Unsolved mysteries)
  Includes bibliographical references.
  ISBN 978-1-61783-301-4
  1. Cooper, D. B.--Juvenile literature. 2. Hijacking of aircraft--
United States--Case studies--Juvenile literature. I. Title.
  HE9803.Z7H556 2012
  364.15'52092--dc23

                                    2011039554

R0428042981

Table of Contents

Hijack!

It was the day before Thanksgiving, November 24, 1971. Thanksgiving is one of the busiest travel seasons of the year, and the crowds at the Portland, Oregon, airport proved that this year was no exception. A line of people formed at the Northwest Orient Airlines ticket counter, ready to purchase tickets for Flight 305. The flight had originated in Washington DC that morning and had made stops in Minnesota, Montana, and Washington. Soon it would land in Portland for its last flight of the day, a short hop to Seattle, Washington.

A man waited in line to purchase his $20 ticket to Seattle. Later, the Federal Bureau of Investigation (FBI) released the following:

> The two flight attendants who spent the most time with him on the plane were interviewed separately the same night in separate cities and gave nearly identical descriptions. They both said he was about 5'10" to 6' [1.78 to 1.8 m], 170 to 180 pounds [77 to 82 kg], in his mid-40s, with brown eyes. People on the ground who came into contact with him also gave very similar descriptions.[1]

The man was neatly dressed in a dark suit, white shirt, and a black tie with a mother-of-pearl tie clip. He wore loafers and a black raincoat. He probably looked like any other businessman traveling through an airport, and no one thought twice about him. He paid for his ticket in cash and gave his name as Dan Cooper. He was not required to show photo

This sketch of Dan Cooper was created from witness accounts.

A POLITE HIJACKER: The crew later described Dan Cooper as "not nervous," "rather nice," and "never cruel or nasty."[2]

identification. He then boarded the airplane and found his seat in Row 18, the last row on the plane. The plane itself was not very full, despite the upcoming holiday, with a total of only 37 passengers. The crew anticipated a quick and uneventful flight.

Dan Cooper asked for a drink—a whiskey and 7-Up—and then took out a pack of Raleigh brand cigarettes. He took one out and lit it, slowly exhaling cigarette smoke into the cabin.

D. B. or Dan?

The name "D. B. Cooper" was nothing more than a mistake. The FBI's search for Cooper included checking the records of known felons named Dan Cooper, in case the hijacker had been careless enough to use his own name. They sent an agent to Portland, Oregon, to check with the local police about a man named D. B. Cooper. A reporter for a news service heard the FBI had been there and asked the clerk, who told him they were investigating "D. B. Cooper." The reporter used the name in his story, and even though the Portland man was cleared, the name D. B. Cooper stuck with the hijacker.

"Miss, I Have a Bomb"

Flight attendant Florence Schaffner

brought Cooper
his drink. As the
plane began taxiing
down the runway,
he paid for it and
also handed her
a note. Schaffner
sat beside him for
takeoff. She was
used to having
passengers flirt
with her, so she
put the note in
her purse without
even reading it.

Hijack

Where did the term *hijack* come
from? It may have originated during
the Prohibition years (1920–1933)
when alcohol was illegal and hijacking
meant seizing a boat or a truck filled
with liquor and stealing it. Back then,
hijacking usually took place between
two rival gangs. It may have come
from a holdup man brandishing a gun
and saying, "Stick 'em up high, Jack,"
which eventually shortened to "High,
Jack." After the end of Prohibition, the
term *hijack* was used for any illegal
takeover of a vehicle. The takeover
of an airplane was first referred to
as *skyjacking*, but *hijack* is more
commonly used to describe it.

However, Cooper motioned for her to read it. When
Schaffner unfolded it, the note said that Cooper had
a bomb in his briefcase and that he was hijacking the
plane. The exact wording of the note is not known
because Cooper took it with him when he left the
plane.

Cooper opened his briefcase and motioned for
Schaffner to look inside. "I was scared to death and
pretty nervous," she later said, "but I do remember
seeing a red cylinder in the suitcase."[3] Cooper then
told Schaffner to write down his demands, which

included $200,000 in cash in a knapsack, as well as two back and two front parachutes. He demanded the plane be refueled when they landed in Seattle and said that if there was any attempt to stop him, he would blow up the plane.

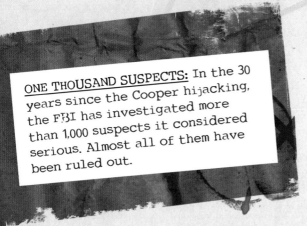

ONE THOUSAND SUSPECTS: In the 30 years since the Cooper hijacking, the FBI has investigated more than 1,000 suspects it considered serious. Almost all of them have been ruled out.

Schaffner took the note to the captain in the cockpit, also alerting another flight attendant, Tina Mucklow. Mucklow went to sit beside Cooper, to keep an eye on him and to try to keep the other passengers safe. She said of him, "He was always polite to me. He did seem impatient at times, though."[4] Schaffner took the note to the pilots. She would continue to relay Cooper's instructions to the flight crew, using the airplane's intercom system.

Meanwhile the captain, William Scott, read the note and contacted Northwest Orient officials on the radio. After telling them of the situation, he put the plane into a holding pattern, circling above Seattle for more than an hour while officials on the ground contacted federal authorities and scurried to collect the money from several area banks. Officials decided to give Cooper the money as 10,000 $20 bills, hoping that the bulk of that much cash might slow down his escape. The money was also photographed before it was given to Cooper so that officials could trace the serial numbers if it was spent in the future. Parachutes were collected from McChord Air Force Base (AFB) nearby.

On the Ground

Captain Scott did not want the other passengers on Flight 305 to panic, so he made excuses about waiting for a runway to be cleared before they could land. Finally, at 5:24 p.m., the air traffic controllers

In the middle of the hijacking, the plane landed in Seattle to refuel and pick up the money and other items Cooper demanded.

McChord AFB

In February 2010, the McChord AFB, which provided the parachutes for Cooper, merged with US Army Fort Lewis. At the time of the Cooper hijacking, it was the home of several squadrons of airplanes. McChord is located approximately ten miles (11 km) south of Tacoma, Washington, and 40 miles (64 km) south of Seattle. Schaffner reported that Cooper looked out his window on the aircraft and correctly pointed out McChord AFB and the city of Tacoma, indicating that he was familiar with the area.

radioed Scott that everything was ready and he could land. When the plane touched down, it taxied to an area brightly lit by floodlights, rather than to the terminal gate as usual. Cooper demanded that the interior cabin lights be extinguished, in case there were police snipers outside ready to target him. The passengers were annoyed at the delay in getting off the plane, but they never realized that a hijacking had taken place on their flight.

Once the plane had landed and a rolling staircase was brought, Mucklow made several trips up and down the staircase, meeting the courier who had the $200,000. Mucklow later described the bag holding the money as "a soft, white, cloth laundry bag," and added that it was open at the top and had no drawstrings to close it.[5] She brought the parachutes on board also and showed everything to Cooper for his approval.

Cooper then allowed the 36 other passengers, Schaffner, and another flight attendant to leave the plane in Seattle. He sent Mucklow forward and told her, "Go to the front, pull the curtain (between the coach and first class compartments), and don't come back."[6] Mucklow then joined the pilots in the cockpit. Captain Scott later remarked, "Everything seemed to go nicely as long as we went along with (the hijacker's) demands."[7] Neither he nor any other crew member attempted to stop the hijacking. Instead, they followed the direction of the Northwest Orient officials on the ground and complied with Cooper's demands.

As the plane finished refueling, Cooper demanded that they fly him to Mexico. The captain informed

Paul Cini

Eleven days before the Cooper hijacking, a man named Paul Cini hijacked an Air Canada flight from Calgary in Alberta, Canada. Cini, armed with bundles of dynamite and a shotgun, wore a black mask over his head and threatened to blow up the passengers and crew. The passengers were safely released in Great Falls, Montana. He held the crew hostage for eight hours, demanding money and a parachute, but when he set his gun down in order to put on the parachute, the flight crew tackled and disarmed him. FBI officials suspect Cooper may have copied his plan for the hijacking from Cini.

him the trip would require another refueling stop in Reno, Nevada, which Cooper did not comment on. He did not request a specific flight route. As the plane climbed into the night sky above Seattle, the crew wondered what was going to happen next, and if the hijacking would take a turn for the worse.

The passengers were allowed to safely leave the plane, and no one was injured.

Chapter 2

An Era of Trust

The hijacking of Northwest Orient Flight 305 came at a time when US society was changing, and yet some aspects—such as the airlines—still seemed to exist in a time of trust. Bob Dylan's song "The Times They Are a Changin'" was a good motto for the United States in the late 1960s and early 1970s. People were beginning to protest the war in Vietnam and damage to the environment and to express hostility toward government and big business. Many of the traditional values such as home, family, democracy, and capitalism were being questioned. The old honor systems were dissolving, and society seemed less law-abiding and trustworthy.

But despite the changes in society, things had not changed very much in the airline industry, which was still based on trust. Passengers and baggage were not routinely searched or screened before entering a plane. Smoking was allowed in every part of the airplane. Passengers were not required to show photo identification before boarding, and there were no metal detectors.

Early stewardesses were hired for their attractiveness and glamour.

At this point in time, flight attendants were still called stewardesses and were generally women. They were required to meet specific height and weight guidelines and to be attractive, which often meant they received unwanted attention from male passengers. This is why Schaffner was suspicious of Cooper's motives when he first passed her the note. She figured he was just another overly attentive male passenger.

Between 1968 and 1972, hijackings became more frequent on many airline flights all over the world. And one hijacking often led to another, as so-called copycat hijackers used others' ideas to carry out their own hijackings. Hijackings tended to fall into two categories: transportation and extortion. Some hijackers wanted to be taken to another country. Others used hijacking as a way to extort money or to free political prisoners or accomplish other political goals. Most of the earlier hijackings in the United States were

COPYCATS: In 1972 alone, 15 copycat hijackings used the same method Cooper used. However, all of the hijackers were eventually apprehended. Only Cooper managed to avoid capture by the authorities.

A Cuban refugee hijacked this plane in 1968 and forced it to fly to Havana. All the passengers returned to the United States safely.

transportation hijackings, and in an overwhelming number of cases, the hijackers demanded transportation either to or from Cuba. The first true extortion hijacking in the United States took place in June 1970, when a man named Arthur Barkley held an entire plane hostage at the Dulles Airport near Washington DC and demanded $100 million from

A Samurai Hijacking

One of the oddest methods of hijacking took place on March 31, 1970. A group of Japanese student dissidents used samurai swords and daggers to hijack a plane at the Tokyo, Japan, airport. They were members of the Japan Red Army faction and demanded to be flown to North Korea. According to a newspaper report, "The militant students . . . refused to let any of the passengers leave the plane or anyone else to enter. Television broadcasts by cameras zoomed into the cockpit with telephoto lenses showed occasional glimpses of a student with a short samurai sword standing behind crew members."[1] The students were taken to North Korea, where the government gave them asylum. None of the passengers were injured.

the government. He was eventually overpowered by airline personnel.

Law in the Sky

In September 1970, Palestinian terrorists hijacked four planes— two of them American—and threatened to destroy them if their demands were not met. In response to this incident, President Richard Nixon mandated that undercover sky marshals would now be required on select flights in order to deter potential hijackings. At first, people were not aware that sky marshals might be present on certain flights. This worked in the marshals' favor, since potential hijackers were also unaware of the presence of these law enforcement officials. The marshals themselves had to learn to distinguish between the behavior of potential hijackers and the regular behavior of passengers for whom flying was a novelty, as demonstrated in this account from David Leach, one of the first sky marshals:

> *A lot of people were fascinated with the fact that there was a lavatory onboard an airplane. In those days, the lavatory was at the front of the airplane adjacent to the cockpit door. And these people would walk down the aisle; they'd grab the cockpit door and start shaking it. And my partner and I, we'd put our hands on our guns and look at each other and say, 'Oh no. Don't tell me this is it. This is it. The guy's trying to get into the cockpit.' And then they'd inevitably see the sign 'Lavatory,' go in there, and we'd just kind of sit back and say, 'Wow.'*[2]

But even the presence of sky marshals did not stop hijackings. In December 1972, the Federal Aviation Administration (FAA) announced that all airlines had one month

Lockerbie

It took another airline tragedy in 1988 to convince the FAA to start screening passengers' radios and other portable devices. On December 21, a Pan-Am Airlines jumbo jet with 258 people on board exploded and then crashed onto the Scottish town of Lockerbie. All passengers and crew on board—as well as 11 people in the town—were killed. It was later determined that the bomb was planted by terrorists with links to Libya.

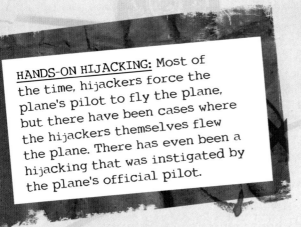

HANDS-ON HIJACKING: Most of the time, hijackers force the plane's pilot to fly the plane, but there have been cases where the hijackers themselves flew the plane. There has even been a hijacking that was instigated by the plane's official pilot.

to put procedures in place for searching passengers and baggage. The first metal detectors were actually adapted from the logging industry, which used metal detectors to find metal in logs that might damage the saw in the sawmill. Leach describes the first passenger metal detectors:

> Some of them were like tunnels, like 4 or 5 ft [1.2 or 1.5 m] long, and they had to walk up a little ramp and down a little ramp. And we used to watch people fall into them and watch people fall out of them. It was really strange.[3]

Passengers complained about the new rules. Some were afraid the metal detectors were hazardous to their health until it was shown the machines gave off less radiation than the glowing dial on a wristwatch. Others complained that the machines violated their Fourth Amendment rights against illegal searches and seizures, but this assertion was defeated since the searches were applied to everyone and could not be used as a form of discrimination.

Still, for some people, it completely changed the way they felt about air travel. According to Dennis O'Madigan with Piedmont Airlines,

> *Many people considered the airlines to be kind of romantic. The meal service was good. People dressed in suits or in dresses. So now that people realized they were going to have to submit themselves and their bags and anything else they brought on the plane to search, that did not*

This early metal detector was installed at La Guardia Airport in New York City in 1971.

enhance the early [1960s] romantic approach that the passenger had when they boarded an airplane.[4]

Despite instituting these new security procedures, hijackings continued. In addition, terrorism became a bigger fear. In 1988, the FAA began looking more closely at passengers' portable computers and radios. Baggage was no longer allowed on a plane unless it belonged to a specific passenger.

Cooper and the November 1971 Northwest Hijacking, or NORJAK, certainly contributed to a changing attitude about air safety

Terrorism and Hijacking

One of the most dramatic and deadly incidents of airline hijacking took place on September 11, 2001. On that day, terrorists hijacked four separate flights in the eastern United States. Two of these airplanes were flown into two towers of New York City's World Trade Center, ultimately destroying them. One was flown into the Pentagon in Washington DC. The fourth flight was likely headed for either the White House or the US Capitol building, but it instead crash-landed in a field in Shanksville, Pennsylvania. Thousands of people died as a result of these hijackings. The 9/11 attacks were intended as terrorist acts, but most hijackings are performed as a way to demand money or draw attention to political situations.

Since the terror attacks of September 11, 2001, many countries have initiated new hijacking policies. They have trained military pilots to shoot down commercial airliners if it seems likely they will be crashed into target buildings.

and security measures. But as Flight 305 climbed into the air above Seattle, those precautions were in the future, and Cooper fully expected that his hijacking demands would be met and he would escape.

The September 11, 2001, attacks were the most deadly hijackings ever, with more than 3,000 total casualties.

Chapter 3

Flight 305

The crew on Flight 305 dealt with Cooper's demands as best they could. The pilot, Captain William Scott, had 20 years of flight experience. Also on board were a first officer and a flight engineer, neither of whom ever saw Cooper or communicated directly with him. The flight attendants were all in their early 20s, but as part of their training, they had been taught how to deal with difficult and even potentially dangerous passengers. When Mucklow first sat down beside Cooper in the airplane, she attempted to talk to him and possibly to keep him from harming or threatening other passengers. Even the mere knowledge that a hijacking was underway could cause the other passengers to panic and send the situation out of control. Following their training, both Mucklow and Schaffner had kept the other passengers from realizing that anything was wrong, and the captain's announcements over the intercom were deliberately bland and misleading, claiming air traffic delays as the reason for circling the Seattle airport.

Mucklow and other members of the flight crew speak to the FBI hours after the attack.

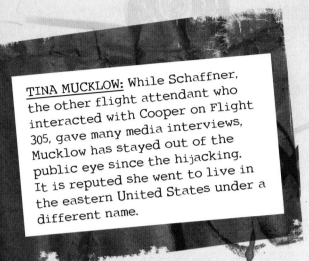

TINA MUCKLOW: While Schaffner, the other flight attendant who interacted with Cooper on Flight 305, gave many media interviews, Mucklow has stayed out of the public eye since the hijacking. It is reputed she went to live in the eastern United States under a different name.

Once the rest of the passengers and two of the flight attendants were safely off the plane, it was up to Mucklow and the pilot to keep Cooper calm and to prevent any injuries. It is most likely due to their training and their ability to remain calm that there was no violence involved in the hijacking.

Underway

While the aircraft was being refueled in Seattle, the FAA asked Cooper for a face-to-face meeting on board the plane, but he refused. Refueling took longer than it should have due to a problem with the tanker truck pumping mechanism, which made Cooper suspicious. Cooper examined the first four parachutes that were brought to him, which had come from McChord AFB. He rejected them, and officials then obtained four new parachutes from a nearby skydiving school instead. Cooper accepted these. As the three tankers finished refueling the aircraft, Cooper also examined the money and was ready to depart.

As the plane left Seattle into a winter storm, Cooper told the pilot he needed to fly toward Mexico. He also instructed him to fly no higher than 10,000 feet (3,000 m), maintain the minimum airspeed possible without stalling the aircraft, and have the wing flaps at 15 degrees and the landing gear down. Cooper's familiarity with the aircraft and what conditions are necessary for parachuting has led to the assumption that he either had military skydiving experience or was an airline employee.

As the plane left Seattle, two F-106 fighter aircraft took off from McChord AFB, following the Boeing 727 at a distance so Cooper would not see them. A National Guard plane on a training mission was also diverted to follow the Cooper plane, but it had to turn back after running low on fuel.

As Cooper sent Mucklow to the forward compartment, she glanced back and thought she saw

One of the parachutes Cooper requested

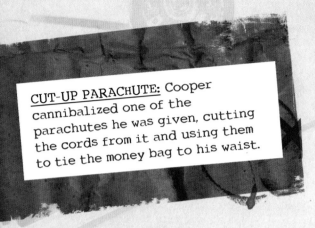

CUT-UP PARACHUTE: Cooper cannibalized one of the parachutes he was given, cutting the cords from it and using them to tie the money bag to his waist.

him use part of what looked like parachute cord to tie something around his waist. She assumed it was the money bag.

Approximately 30 minutes later, a warning light in the cockpit showed that the rear stairway was being opened. Unlike larger planes, the Boeing 727 had a rear stairway—called the airstair—that could be opened from beneath the tail of the aircraft both before and during flight. This allowed passengers to enter and exit the plane without needing an airport gate or portable stairs to be brought to the aircraft. Planes with larger or higher bodies could not use airstairs because the stairs would be too long to be practical. Cooper had initially asked the pilot to take off from Seattle with the rear exit door open and the airstair extended, but the Northwest Orient home office told the crew it was unsafe to take off that way. Cooper argued, saying he knew it was safe, but he let the crew proceed. When the light in the cockpit indicated that the airstair was fully extended, Captain Scott activated the intercom system and asked, "Is everything okay back there? Anything we can do for you?" The witnesses reported that Cooper yelled "No!"[1] This was the last communication the crew had with him.

Gone

At approximately 8:11 p.m., a few minutes after their last exchange with Cooper, the crew felt bumps as the aircraft jolted and dipped. The FBI later determined that these were most likely caused by Cooper jumping, which forced the airstair to snap shut momentarily before reopening. The jolting was strong enough that the pilot had to take measures to bring the plane back to level flying.

The plane was flying through adverse weather conditions, with strong winds and freezing rain, and a temperature of approximately seven degrees Fahrenheit below zero (-22°C). Even an experienced skydiver would avoid jumping in a storm similar to the one Cooper disappeared into, especially wearing only a suit, coat, and loafers, with no helmet, gloves,

The arrow indicates the location of the airstair on a 727.

The Cooper Vane

Cooper's hijacking resulted in a new safety feature for any aircraft with a rear stairway. Called the "Cooper Vane," the device is a mechanical wedge, activated by airflow over the outside of the airplane, which prevents the stairway from being lowered while the plane is in flight. After three hijackings took place using Cooper's method of deploying the rear stairs and parachuting out of the plane, the FAA ordered the Cooper Vane to be installed on all Boeing 727 aircraft.

mask, or goggles. Cooper jumped into the darkness, in a place where he could not see the ground and over terrain that was forested and mountainous. This, along with the fact that he did not give the pilot a specific route to follow as he flew to Reno, was a clue that he had not arranged to land in a specific place or to meet an accomplice.

Life magazine ran this image of a 727 in flight with an open airstair on its August 11, 1972, cover.

LIFE
The Secret Bobby Fischer

Escape route for a skyjacker—the rear hatch on a Braniff jet. Airline has now sealed hatches on its 727s

SKYJACKING
The get-tough policy could make it even worse

AUGUST 11 · 1972 · 50¢

The airstair remained down as the plane approached Reno. The crew continued to page Cooper on the intercom with no response, and once Flight 305 landed in Reno, FBI agents, local police, and other officials surrounded it. An armed search of the plane quickly confirmed that Cooper was, indeed, gone.

Cooper Spotted?

In 1985, a woman named Janet (who refused to give a last name so as to avoid unwelcome publicity) recounted an incident that allegedly occurred the night of the hijacking, as she was leaving her house with her family. As told in the Ogden *Standard Examiner*:

Janet, who was in the passenger seat, looked up just as the car was backing out of the driveway and saw a light pass overhead. A platform or ladder below a plane caught her eye. "What I saw was flames and thought I saw something on the platform which could have been a person," Janet said. Immediately, the fireball arched away from the platform, split into two and then disappeared in the direction of the Columbia River.[2]

The private investigator who interviewed Janet believed that she had seen Cooper light the bundle of road flares—the same ones he had had inside his briefcase, which could have been made to look like a bomb—in order to judge the wind direction and guide him to the ground. However, Janet's account has never been officially verified by the FBI.

Chapter 4

The Hunt Is On

Cooper left very few clues behind when he parachuted out of Flight 305: his skinny black tie and a tie clip, eight cigarette butts, two of the four parachutes he had demanded, and his saliva on the glass that he drank from during the flight. The saliva, which today could be used to extract a DNA sample, was of no use in 1971 when DNA testing was not yet widely available. However, years later, when the FBI reopened the Cooper case, they were able to get a DNA sample from his tie. There were fingerprints all over the cabin of the airplane, and 66 of them were never identified.

Three items collected by law enforcement include Cooper's airplane ticket, his tie, and his tie clip.

However, the FBI could not find a set that was clearly Cooper's.

A Needle in a Haystack

One of the first things the FBI tried to establish in its investigation of the NORJAK incident was where Cooper might have landed. It was difficult to pinpoint a search area because there were so many variables involved.

DNA Testing

DNA testing was not possible until the late 1970s and early 1980s. Before that, scientists could only use methods such as blood type for situations in which tissues and blood needed to be checked for compatibility, such as during an organ transplant. No reliable method existed for determining identity or relationships through blood testing. Now DNA is used to identify individuals and even their relatives with amazing accuracy. It is routinely used in crimes to identify suspects from tiny amounts of their DNA left in hairs, skin samples, or saliva.

The aircraft's speed at the moment of the jump, as well as the environmental conditions the plane was traveling through (which could vary depending on location and altitude) would all have affected where Cooper landed. Even the time it took Cooper to pull the ripcord on his parachute could have affected his landing position. Visibility was also limited because of darkness and the storm, so the air force pilots who were following the plane did not see anything leave the plane, either visually or on radar. But if a figure dressed in dark clothing left the airplane, it is not likely he would have been seen.

The FBI were also certain that Cooper did not have an accomplice on the ground, since it would have been almost impossible to coordinate. Cooper would have had to instruct the crew to fly on a specific flight path, and he would have needed to know exactly when they were over a specific drop zone so he could jump at the right moment. But Cooper did not do any of this. He just told the pilot to fly to Mexico.

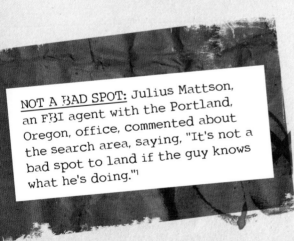

NOT A BAD SPOT: Julius Mattson, an FBI agent with the Portland, Oregon, office, commented about the search area, saying, "It's not a bad spot to land if the guy knows what he's doing."¹

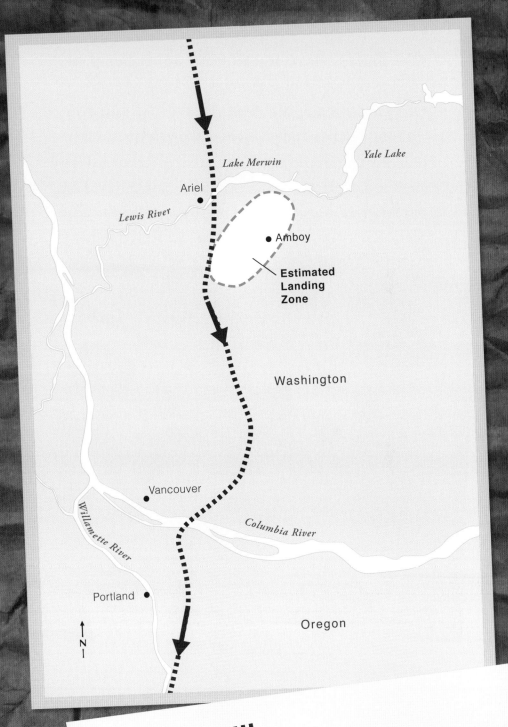

Yale Lake

Lake Merwin

Ariel

Lewis River

Amboy

Estimated
Landing
Zone

Washington

Vancouver

Willamette River

Columbia River

Portland

Oregon

N

Path of Flight 305

The FBI finally established a search area of 28 square miles (73 sq km), south of Lake Merwin near the town of Ariel, Washington. The actual manhunt had to be postponed several days until the weather improved. The searchers included FBI agents and sheriffs' deputies and took place on foot, in helicopters, and in patrol boats on Lake Merwin

Law enforcement searched for Cooper from the air in helicopters.

and nearby Yale Lake. They found areas with broken treetops and sighted several pieces of plastic that looked like parachutes from the air but turned out to be unrelated to the hijacking.

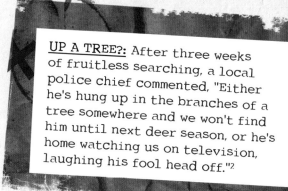

UP A TREE?: After three weeks of fruitless searching, a local police chief commented, "Either he's hung up in the branches of a tree somewhere and we won't find him until next deer season, or he's home watching us on television, laughing his fool head off."[2]

After several days of searching, no trace of Cooper or any of his equipment was found.

Ralph Himmelsbach, an agent with the FBI who worked on the Cooper case for years, later found out from the Flight 305 pilot that the aircraft's position might not have been where they thought it was when the first search area was established. Because planes did not have satellite tracking in 1971 and their flight plans were not tracked as precisely, the pilot had actually been traveling farther east than anyone realized at the time. It meant that the searchers on the ground were probably looking outside of the actual drop zone.

A Money Trail?

In late 1971, the FBI released the serial numbers of the $20 bills that were given to Cooper, which

Web sites allow the public to check the serial number of any $20 bill against a database of the Cooper ransom serial numbers.

had been photographed before they were delivered to the airplane. They distributed these numbers to banks and other financial institutions and to law enforcement agencies all over the world. Northwest Orient Airlines offered 15 percent of the cash as a reward to anyone who found it. The serial numbers were also released to the general public. Later, two local newspapers, the Seattle *Post-Intelligencer* and the Oregon *Journal*, also republished the serial numbers and offered rewards for anyone who turned in one of the bills.

Dead or Alive?

In 1972, after spring had thawed the ground, the FBI launched another series of searches. For 18 days in March, and again in April, army

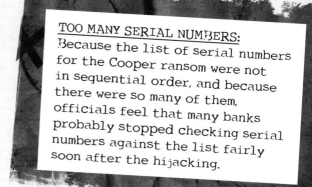

TOO MANY SERIAL NUMBERS: Because the list of serial numbers for the Cooper ransom were not in sequential order, and because there were so many of them, officials feel that many banks probably stopped checking serial numbers against the list fairly soon after the hijacking.

soldiers from Fort Lewis, air force personnel, civilian volunteers, and National Guard members conducted ground searches of the area. A marine salvage firm even used a submarine to search Lake Merwin. But none of the searches turned up any clues about Cooper.

Several experts began theorizing that Cooper had not survived the jump from the airplane, due to his inexperience as a skydiver. Years after the hijacking, when the FBI reopened its case file on Cooper, an FBI agent commented on its Web site:

We originally thought Cooper was an experienced jumper, perhaps even a paratrooper. We concluded after a few years this was simply not true. No experienced parachutist would have jumped in the pitch-black night, in the rain, with a 200-mile-an-hour [320-km/h] wind in his face, wearing loafers and a trench coat. It was simply too risky. He also missed that his reserve chute was only for training and had been sewn shut—something a skilled skydiver would have checked. . . . Diving into the wilderness without a plan, without the right equipment, in such terrible conditions, he probably never even got his chute open.[3]

Himmelsbach agrees that Cooper most likely did not survive the jump:

Test Jump

As part of the investigation into where Cooper might have landed, authorities conducted an experimental jump from another 727 aircraft. They followed the same flight plan, and Captain Scott flew the plane. There was also a heavy rainstorm, similar to the night of the hijacking. FBI agents then pushed a 200 pound (90 kg) sled from the airstair, and it created the same upward motion of the plane the crew felt during the hijacking. Using this information, they determined that Cooper most likely jumped at 8:13 p.m.

Cooper planned his caper well, but not well enough. He picked the right plane—the only jet in which the stairwell could be opened in mid-flight. . . . But he left the plane with the two worst parachutes, including one marked with an "X," meaning it wouldn't open properly. . . . And he did not ask for warm clothing, a helmet and goggles. "We would have

given it to him; we gave him everything else,"
Himmelsbach says. "He was wearing loafers on
his feet and you know those things blew off the
second he jumped."[4]

Cooper had jumped from Flight 305 into the
blackness of a stormy November night. No one
knew for sure if he had survived the fall or died in
the attempt. But the case was not over, and it would
not be long before another crime occurred, with
startlingly similar details.

Chapter 5

A Copycat Crime . . . or Cooper?

The FBI had no luck in finding any trace of Cooper's whereabouts. Although his trail had been cold from the start, there was still plenty of hope that he would eventually be apprehended. But in an era of frequent hijackings, it was not long before the FBI had to turn its attention to another case, one with some startling similarities.

Flight 855

It was April 7, 1972, on board a routine United Airlines flight from Newark, New Jersey, to Los Angeles, California. The aircraft was another Boeing 727, carrying 85 passengers and six flight-crew members. The plane had just finished a brief stop in Denver, Colorado, and was again airborne when a passenger noticed a man holding something suspicious. It looked like a hand grenade. According to the FBI:

> *A stewardess, notified of the situation, immediately advised the captain. An off-duty pilot known to be on board as a passenger was requested to discreetly walk around and assess the situation only to have the person in question draw a pistol as he approached. The gunman handed over a sealed envelope, labeled "hijack instructions," and stated, "Give this envelope to the girl and have her take it to the captain." A stewardess*

The hijacked 727

complied, and the off-duty pilot returned to his seat.[1]

The entire episode happened so quickly that most of the other passengers were never aware anything was going on. The captain and his crew discussed the situation and decided they would land in Grand Junction, Colorado, where they could radio for law enforcement help. The captain then went on the intercom and told the passengers they were experiencing a small mechanical problem and would be landing soon.

Then the captain finally opened the envelope the hijacker had given to the flight attendant. Inside he found two pages of detailed

The hand grenade used in the copycat hijacking was a toy, and the pistol was unloaded.

46

instructions, as well as a bullet and the pin to the hand grenade, which is the safety device usually installed in a grenade to keep it from exploding. The pin in the envelope implied that the hijacker could detonate the grenade at any time. The instructions told the pilot to land at San Francisco International Airport in California. They also specified how many people could approach the airplane, as well as how far any vehicle other than a refueling truck needed to stay away from the aircraft. Finally, the hijacker demanded $500,000 in cash, four parachutes, and the return of the instructions.

San Francisco

The pilot and his crew decided that the wisest thing to do would be to comply with the hijacker's instructions, so instead of landing in Grand Junction, they changed course for San Francisco. The pilot again told the passengers that Grand Junction had been unable to handle the necessary repairs and that they would have to divert to San Francisco. At the same time, with the safety of everyone on Flight 855 in mind, United Airlines decided to meet the hijacker's demands.

The plane landed, and, following the hijacker's instructions, two flight bags loaded with the money as well as four parachutes were delivered to the plane.

In addition, the hijacker gave the airline personnel his baggage check and had his bags brought up into the plane. The plane was refueled. After three hours on the ground, the hijacker released all of the other passengers and one of the flight attendants. The rest of the crew was ordered into the cockpit, and the plane once again took off.

According to the FBI, the hijacker's messages, which were handwritten, were sent to the cockpit using the flight attendant as a messenger. His instructions told the pilot to fly east, climb to an altitude of 16,000 feet (4,877 m), and fly at exactly 200 miles per hour (322 km/h). The flight path would pass over several specific towns in Utah. He also ordered the crew to depressurize the cabin and warned them that he had a bomb he would detonate if he saw any pursuit planes. He then made careful preparations before jumping:

PEEPHOLE: Another modification that became standard on aircraft after the Cooper hijacking was a peephole installed in the cockpit door. This allowed the flight crew to observe what was going on in the passenger cabin without leaving the cockpit.

The hijacker opened his luggage and covered the peephole between the cockpit and cabin.

48

Observed by [the second officer] through a slight space under the cockpit door, the hijacker quickly put on a jumpsuit, helmet, and parachute. Once he had shut off the cabin lights to better view the ground, the gunman demanded to be kept abreast of wind, ground, and air speeds; altimeter settings; and sky conditions.[2]

The situation continued to feel more than a bit familiar as the messages from the hijacker suddenly ceased and the flight attendant went back into the passenger section of the plane. She discovered that the hijacker had indeed parachuted from the plane somewhere over Utah. The plane landed safely in Salt Lake City, Utah, and, once again, the FBI did a thorough sweep of the aircraft, taking with them

Out of Control

According to an article in *Parachutist*, the hijacker's fall from the plane was not easy. The article's author envisions what that fall would have been like, based on interviews with the hijacker:

He felt as if he were falling from a tall building. Then the blast of freezing air hit. [The hijacker] later said that it practically tore his head off. He arched and got into a belly-to-earth position, but something was wrong. He was in a spin. The heavy duffle bag dangling between his legs had shifted left, and he could not counter the effect. He became weak, dizzy, nauseous, and even blacked out momentarily. When he regained consciousness, he was still spinning, but he fought to control it by leaning his body toward the bag. This only made the spin faster and more violent.[3]

any possible clues, evidence, and fingerprints, including one of the hijacker's handwritten notes. A ground search was conducted in the vicinity of Provo, Utah, since evidence showed the hijacker had probably parachuted into that area.

"A Foolproof Plan"

The FBI did not find the hijacker during their search, but as the news of the hijacking was broadcast

Richard McCoy was caught and tried for the Flight 855 hijacking.

to the public, they received information that led to an arrest. An acquaintance of a man named Richard McCoy Jr. called in with a tip, saying that McCoy had claimed he had a foolproof plan for hijacking an airplane.

McCoy, age 29, seemed to have the ability to parachute from a plane after a hijacking. He was a Vietnam War veteran, a helicopter pilot, an experienced skydiver, and a member of the Utah Air National Guard. He was also known to be having serious financial trouble.

Catching a Hijacker

An FBI brief narrates how McCoy was caught:

"On April 9, [1972] a federal complaint was filed charging McCoy with aircraft piracy and interfering with flight crew members. Later the same day an arrest warrant was obtained and McCoy was taken into custody by FBI agents at his Provo home. Agents examined the accused's home under a search warrant and uncovered various articles of skydiving equipment, an electric typewriter (with key impressions matching those on the typed hijacking instructions), and $499,970 in U.S. currency. A federal grand jury in Salt Lake City indicted McCoy on April 14."[4]

The evidence quickly piled up. The army provided a sample of McCoy's handwriting, as well as his fingerprints, and they both matched the hijacker's handwritten note and the prints he had left on a

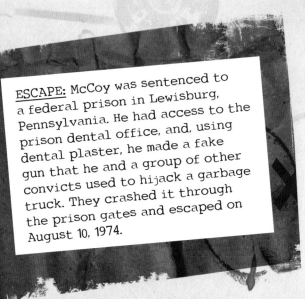

ESCAPE: McCoy was sentenced to a federal prison in Lewisburg, Pennsylvania. He had access to the prison dental office, and, using dental plaster, he made a fake gun that he and a group of other convicts used to hijack a garbage truck. They crashed it through the prison gates and escaped on August 10, 1974.

flight magazine on board the airplane. Soon eyewitnesses came forward and pinpointed McCoy's whereabouts after the hijacking.

McCoy was tried, convicted, and sentenced to 45 years in prison for the hijacking. In 1974, however, he escaped from prison after stealing a garbage truck and breaking through the prison gates. The FBI located him in Virginia three months later, resulting in a standoff. McCoy was killed in the confrontation. But his story—especially with so many similarities to the Cooper hijacking—did not end there.

"I Shot D. B. Cooper"

FBI agent Nicholas O'Hara killed McCoy. He also firmly believed that McCoy and Cooper were the same person and that McCoy had learned from the first hijacking and improved his method for the second hijacking, including acquiring appropriate clothing for the jump. He also claimed that the tie and tie clip left on board the airplane after the Cooper hijacking were later positively identified by McCoy's family as belonging to him. O'Hara said, "When I shot Richard McCoy, I shot D. B. Cooper at the same time."[5] When investigators asked if he was Cooper, McCoy replied, "I don't want to talk to you about it."[6]

In 1991, parole officer Bernie Rhodes and former FBI agent Russell Calame published a book entitled *D. B. Cooper: The Real McCoy*, in which they claim that McCoy and Cooper were the same person. McCoy's widow, Karen McCoy, supposedly admitted later that she had been involved in planning the hijacking, but it was never proven. She later sued the authors of the book, disputing some of their claims. She won, but the authors insisted their account was still valid. And as the search for the identity of Cooper continued, many people were still convinced that McCoy was a likely suspect.

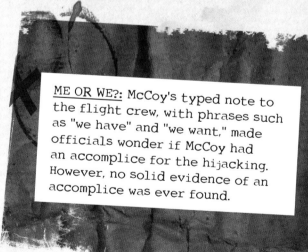

ME OR WE?: McCoy's typed note to the flight crew, with phrases such as "we have" and "we want," made officials wonder if McCoy had an accomplice for the hijacking. However, no solid evidence of an accomplice was ever found.

Chapter 6

Confessions

Richard McCoy was just the first in a long series of people who would become possible suspects in the NORJAK incident. The FBI continued to receive tips about people who may have been Cooper. Several people confessed they were the real D. B. Cooper as they were dying.

Duane Weber

An article in the July 24, 2000, issue of *US News and World Report* broke the story of suspect Duane Weber. In March 1995, Weber was dying of kidney disease in a hospital in Pensacola, Florida. As he became more ill, Weber had something very startling to say:

He called his wife, Jo, to his bed and whispered: "I'm Dan Cooper." Jo, who had learned in 17 years of marriage not to pry too deeply into Duane's past, had no idea what her secretive husband meant. Frustrated, he blurted out: "Oh, let it die with me!" Duane died 11 days later.[1]

Jo had no idea what her husband was talking about, but she was unfamiliar with much of his past. He had been married several times before he had met her. She knew that he had once been in prison and that he had used the name John C. Collins. After Weber's death, Jo took a book out of the library about D. B. Cooper and began reading about him, since she had never heard of the case. The similarities she discovered while reading the book were enough to make her wonder if her husband really had been Cooper. They were similar in height

Handwriting Match?

Jo read about Cooper in a book she checked out from the library. She was surprised to see what looked like her husband's handwriting in the book's margins, although as far as she knew, he never went to the library. On one page, the margin-writer had added the name of the town in Washington where a placard that likely came from the 727 was found. One of Duane's coworkers agreed the handwriting was extremely similar.

and build, both were chain smokers, and the likeness between Weber's photograph and the sketch of Cooper was eerie.

Jo called the FBI immediately after she finished reading the book, but she claimed that they were not initially very interested in her story. But Jo continued to discover things that made her wonder if her husband was indeed the famous hijacker. After his death, she sold his van, and the new owner discovered a wallet hidden inside. It contained a bad conduct discharge from the navy, a social security card, and prison release papers, all in the name of John C. Collins. Jo also remembered seeing a white canvas bag inside a cooler in Duane's van, the same type of bag used for the ransom money. And when they were on vacation in Washington State in 1979, she remembered stopping on the interstate across the Columbia River from the city of Portland. There Duane walked down to the river by himself. Before he died, Weber told his wife that the old knee injury he had was from jumping out of a plane.

Even though the FBI had dismissed her theory, Jo later began talking with Himmelsbach, the FBI agent who had been in charge of the Cooper case until his retirement. He convinced the FBI to open a case file on Duane Weber, and they interviewed Jo

where dredging had disturbed the layers of silt and sand on the riverbanks. However, other specialists argue that the money must have been buried until almost when it was found because the rubber bands had not disintegrated. If the money had been in the river for more than a few months, they argue, the rubber bands would have crumbled away.

Himmelsbach, *center*, with the ransom money and Brian Ingram's parents

The discovery may have been a clue in the Cooper case, but it did not ultimately provide any firm answers about Cooper's fate or where the rest of the money might be. Experts could not agree whether the money had been in the water since the night of the hijacking or if it had come from a hiding place, which would indicate Cooper had survived the fall and handled the money.

For Sale

In 2006, Brian Ingram sold some of the money he had found in the riverbank. The money, as part of Cooper's ransom, had more value as a souvenir than it did at its face value. The bills sold for $37,433. Ingram had been keeping it in a safe deposit box at a local bank. According to an article in the *Arkansas Times*:

"I just think it is time to do something with them," Ingram said. "Our family had time to hold on to them for a while and look back on it. It's just time to let the public know about them." Ingram is selling the entirety of the bills with readable serial numbers, which includes only 15 "whole bills," which are deteriorated around the edges, and 10 "half-bills," which are further gone. He will keep the rest of the money, which amounts to scraps of paper resembling confetti.[6]

More Theories

Meanwhile, the tips and confessions about Cooper continued to accumulate. In 1985, author Max Gunther published the book *D. B. Cooper: What Really Happened*, which is based on the account of a woman who claimed she had found Cooper,

Searchers sift through sand from the riverbank, looking for more money fragments from the Cooper ransom.

A Money Puzzle

In 2006, Brian Ingram asked the staff at Professional Coin Grading Services to examine the money from the Cooper ransom before he put it up for sale. Ingram wanted to have the money professionally certified, which would verify that it came from the Cooper ransom money. It was no easy task to identify bills that had been wet and degrading for years. President Jason Bradford described it:

We were able to carefully separate the submitted notes and fragments that had been affixed together for decades. In some cases, portions of as many as four notes were stuck together due to their apparent long exposure to water and various weather conditions. We also were able to piece together portions of several separate fragments, sort of like a bank note jigsaw puzzle, to make a complete serial number.[7]

injured, two days after the hijacking. According to her account, they fell in love and she kept him hidden. However, most people did not find the account very credible.

In 1986, Himmelsbach published his own book, *NORJAK: The Investigation of D. B. Cooper* with coauthor Thomas Worcester. In it, Himmelsbach argued that Cooper died in the fall from the airplane. His investigations into the hijacking led him to believe that Cooper's skydiving inexperience, lack of proper equipment, and the weather conditions that night would have made survival nearly impossible. But it would just be a few years later when another possible Cooper suspect was identified. The similarities and clues would be hard to dismiss.

"Whatever Cooper would have hit down there, he would have hit hard. Even if he'd just sprained his leg it'd be a death sentence in that kind of environment. I think he got as far as the creek, died, and the spring floods took part of his pack downstream and eventually into the Columbia."[8]
—Agent Ralph Himmelsbach

Chapter 7

A Dead Ringer

Lyle Christiansen, of Morris, Minnesota, was watching an episode of the television show *Unsolved Mysteries* in 2003 about the Cooper hijacking. At one point the famous FBI sketch of Cooper flashed on the screen. Lyle later said,

> I sat up in my chair, because my brother [Kenneth] was a dead ringer to the composite sketch of D. B. . . . There were so many circumstances that I became convinced my brother was truly D. B. Cooper![1]

Lyle suddenly remembered something his brother, Kenneth Christiansen, had told him just before he died of cancer in 1994: "There is something you should know, but I can't tell you . . ."[2]

Bashful in Seattle

Lyle, a retired postal worker, was not sure what to do about his suspicions. He contacted the FBI, but no one there seemed to think his suspicions were valid. In January 2004, he wrote to the FBI, "I'm

Kenneth Christiansen, *right*, compared to a Cooper suspect sketch

The Pursuit

In 1981, a move called *The Pursuit of D. B. Cooper* hit theaters. It starred Treat Williams as Cooper, as well as Robert Duvall as an insurance investigator trying to find Cooper. The movie was loosely based on a 1980 novel, *Free Fall*, written by J. D. Reed. It mostly follows a fictionalized account of Cooper's escape once he reached the ground. The movie has many inaccuracies, such as Cooper leaping from the plane in daylight, when in reality it was nighttime and raining. The movie did not do well. As a publicity stunt for the movie, Universal Pictures offered a reward of $1 million for information that led to the arrest of the real Cooper, but no one ever claimed it.

WHO SAYS
YOU CAN'T TAKE IT
WITH YOU?

THE PURSUIT OF
D.B. COOPER

not getting any younger. . . . Before I die I would like to find out if my brother was D. B. Cooper. From what I know I feel that he *was* and *without a doubt*."[3]

Then he tried contacting author and movie director Nora Ephron with the idea that his brother's story would make a great movie. He wanted to call it "Bashful in Seattle," since Kenneth had lived near Seattle and Ephron had directed the popular movie *Sleepless in Seattle*. But he never heard from

Ephron. He finally wrote to a private investigator in New York, Skipp Porteous, who agreed to look into the case:

> As you know, I have been trying to contact Nora Ephron, but for some reason she doesn't answer my letters. Now I would like you to help me. I am sitting on the answer to a many decades mystery which has never been solved. . . . No one was killed or injured in the caper but could easily have been. . . . I hope you will think about this and let me know.[4]

Porteous was intrigued and began corresponding with Lyle by e-mail. Lyle said at one point, "Yes, I knew the culprit personally. He was my brother."[5] As Porteous began investigating Kenneth Christiansen, he found many elements of Christiansen's life that seemed to fit the 1971 hijacking. Christiansen had been in the US Army in 1944 and trained as a paratrooper and so would have known how to skydive. After leaving the army, he got a job as a purser with Northwest Orient Airlines. The job would have given him familiarity with both the 727 aircraft and the operations of the airline itself.

Christiansen did not mix with other Northwest Orient staff members, and many of them did not

Kenneth Christiansen learned to parachute as a paratrooper during World War II.

even know who he was. He could have traveled on
Flight 305 without being recognized:

> "He was almost invisible," says Harry Honda, a
> Northwest purser who worked with Kenny. "If
> you asked somebody on his plane who was the
> purser on that flight, they couldn't tell you—that's
> how quiet this guy was." If they had a layover,
> Kenny would not go out with the staff. "He was
> noncommunicative," says Mary Patricia Laffey
> Inman, a Northwest purser. "He kept to himself.
> He was a plaid-shirt guy," says Lyle Gehring,
> another Northwest purser, who worked alongside
> Kenny for years. "You ask people and say 'Ken
> Christiansen,' they say, 'Who?'"[6]

Even more interesting was the fact that when
Christiansen died, he had more than $200,000
in his bank accounts, as well as several valuable
collections of gold coins and stamps. He had also
paid cash—$16,500—for his home in Bonney
Lake, Washington, just eight months after the
hijacking. He had previously lived in a small, shabby
apartment in Sumner, Washington. He had also paid
off some old debts and loaned money to a friend's
sister. Northwest Orient was known for its frequent
strikes and layoffs, so its employees could never be
guaranteed a certain wage every month. It seemed
very unlikely that Christiansen could have purchased

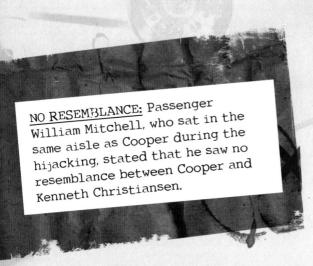

NO RESEMBLANCE: Passenger William Mitchell, who sat in the same aisle as Cooper during the hijacking, stated that he saw no resemblance between Cooper and Kenneth Christiansen.

a house for cash with only his Northwest salary.

Porteous was also intrigued by the other similarities between Christiansen and the NORJAK hijacker. They were both chain smokers and drank bourbon. They were also both left-handed, something investigators had determined from the way the tie clip on the hijacker's tie had been applied. And when Porteous showed a photograph of Christiansen to Schaffner, she thought it resembled the hijacker more than any other suspect's photograph she had seen.

The FBI's Doubts

However, despite the evidence that Porteous and Lyle produced, the FBI still felt there was not enough evidence to seriously link Kenneth Christiansen to Cooper. They pointed out that some of Christiansen's physical characteristics, such as height, weight, and eye color, did not match, since Christiansen was shorter and less heavy than Cooper and also had less hair. Lyle did claim that his brother started wearing a toupee before the hijacking, and then stopped wearing it immediately after.

When Himmelsbach was shown the evidence connecting Christiansen to Cooper, he too was somewhat skeptical about the differences in physical characteristics. He was also convinced that it would have been too difficult for an employee of the airline to carry out a hijacking conspiracy, since they never knew which flight they might be assigned to. He was also convinced that, based on his acquaintance with airline personnel, a lone employee would have too much integrity to hijack his own airline. However, when Geoffrey Gray, researching an article on Christiansen and Cooper for *New York Magazine*, showed him the Christiansen photo, he was more interested. Gray explains,

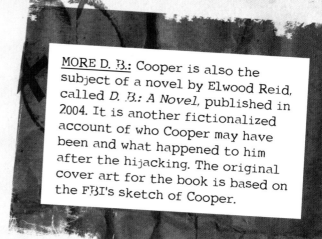

MORE D. B.: Cooper is also the subject of a novel by Elwood Reid, called *D. B.: A Novel*, published in 2004. It is another fictionalized account of who Cooper may have been and what happened to him after the hijacking. The original cover art for the book is based on the FBI's sketch of Cooper.

I pulled out photos of Kenny. He studied them slowly. "Not bad," he said. "Except for the hair." I then showed him Kenny's discharge papers from the Army. . . . "Well, he's too short, not heavy enough, and has got the wrong color eyes," [Himmelsbach commented.] I then told him about Kenny's history: his service in the paratroops, and working for Northwest. . . . "All of this makes him look like a good suspect to me," he said. "If I was still on duty and it were up to me, I'd say, 'This guy is a 'must investigate.'"[7]

Decoded

Brad Meltzer's *Decoded* is a television show that airs on the History Channel. It deals with US conspiracy theories, secret codes, and unsolved mysteries. Meltzer himself writes political thrillers as well as nonfiction. In January 2011, *Decoded* ran a show about D. B. Cooper, in which he and his team investigated the evidence linking Kenneth Christiansen to Cooper. Robert Blevins, author and publisher of the book about Cooper titled *Into the Blast*, was interviewed on the show. During the show's filming, the crew used infrared scanning to scan Christiansen's former house from top to bottom. They discovered a secret hiding space in the attic of this house. Some speculate this might have been where Christiansen hid the ransom money during his lifetime.

Even though the FBI was not interested in Kenneth Christiansen, Porteous and author and publisher Robert Blevins continued investigating the connection. They eventually published a book called *Into the Blast: The*

True Story of D. B. Cooper, in which they conclude that Christiansen was indeed Cooper.

Meanwhile, there were still other theories and suspects surfacing in the D. B. Cooper case, each with its own convincing similarities and arguments.

Chapter 8

A Son's Suspicions

Just before Christmas in 1971, Greg Gossett remembered his father, William Gossett, showing him a large amount of money. Greg remembered being surprised because his father had a gambling problem and never seemed to have enough money. Later, William Gossett would tell his son about his connection with a famous hijacking case:

> *His father told him on his twenty-first birthday that he had hijacked the plane, then revealed to his son two keys to a safety deposit box at a bank in Vancouver, British Columbia, where the money was stored. "He said that I could never tell anybody until*

after he died," Greg Gossett said. Kirk Gossett, another son, says his father also told the story several times. "He had the type of temperament to do something like this," Kirk Gossett said. [1]

Suspicious Details

William Gossett also had a background as a private investigator, specializing in cases involving money fraud, missing persons, and cults. He

NAME CHANGER: There was also evidence that William Gossett (who died in 2003) changed his identity several times after the hijacking. In the mid-1970s, he changed his first name to Wolfgang and became a Catholic priest. During this time, he also grew a mustache and a goatee.

often assisted the FBI with crimes and was actually commended by them for his help in a case involving a woman who had joined a cult.

Gossett was in the US Marines, the Army Air Force, and the US Air Force, and had served during both the Vietnam and Korean Wars. He was also an ROTC instructor. Gossett had a great deal of experience with skydiving. According to Galen Cook, a lawyer who is writing a book about Gossett as the real D. B. Cooper, "He had the level of skills and ability to plan the entire thing with military

A Confession?

According to Cook's investigation, Gossett had commented to one of his wives that he could "write the epitaph for D. B. Cooper."[3] Cook also claims that Gossett had actually confessed to a retired judge in Salt Lake City:

The judge told Galen Cook, "In 1977, he walked into my office and closed the door and said he thought he might be in some trouble, that he was involved in a hijacking in Portland and Seattle a few years ago and that he might have left prints behind. He said he was D. B. Cooper. I told him to keep his mouth shut and don't do anything stupid, and not to bring it up again."[4]

precision, and to not only parachute from the plane but to survive."[2]

Cook collected samples of Gossett's DNA and fingerprints and gave them to the FBI, but the FBI stated there was no firm evidence connecting Gossett to Cooper and that the only links were statements Gossett supposedly made to other people. If Gossett was indeed Cooper, it could not be proved. Gossett remains the only major suspect in the D. B. Cooper case who has not been officially eliminated by the FBI.

D. B. Cooper: Man or Woman?

Meanwhile, another theory had surfaced concerning the identity of Cooper. In 1977, avid pilots Ron and Pat Forman met a woman named Barbara Dayton at an airport near Puyallup, Washington. They quickly became friends. The Formans noticed that Dayton seemed able to do things that, at that time, most women her age did not do. She was an excellent pilot and mechanic and knew a lot about electronics. After they became friends, Dayton told the Formans she had actually spent the first 43 years of her life as a man, Robert Dayton, before having a sex change operation in 1969. Dayton, as a man, had served in the merchant marine and the army during WWII, and although he became a private pilot, he was never able to obtain a commercial pilot's license.

Eventually she also told the Formans that she was Cooper and that she had hijacked the plane to get back at the airline industry, which had prevented her from becoming a pilot because of

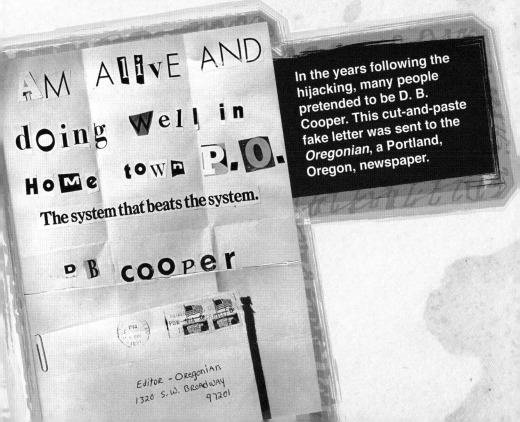

In the years following the hijacking, many people pretended to be D. B. Cooper. This cut-and-paste fake letter was sent to the *Oregonian*, a Portland, Oregon, newspaper.

An Indictment

Why would Cooper, if he was still alive, still be in hiding or concealing his identity so many years after his crime? Because of the statute of limitations, the fifth anniversary of the Cooper hijacking was a serious date for the FBI. The statute of limitations limits the time period in which a person can be tried for a crime. Once that period of time has elapsed, the state can no longer try the defendant for the crime. The government had to get an indictment for the hijacking before the end of the day on November 24, 1976, or else the hijacker might go free even if he was caught later.

The FBI brought the case before a grand jury in Oregon. A so-called John Doe indictment was returned against Cooper. Because no one really knew who Cooper was, the indictment was issued against a John Doe. This started the legal proceedings, so even if Cooper was caught many, many years after his crime, he could still be charged.

their strict rules and conditions. Dayton claimed she had never spent the money, saying it was hidden in a well south of Portland, Oregon. According to an article by Bruce A. Smith:

The Formans say Dayton told them bits and pieces of her famous story over a life-long friendship that began in 1977. . . . The Formans say Dayton donned the supreme disguise by reverting to her male persona to become D. B. Cooper. One indisputable fact is that Barbara Dayton was a highly skilled pilot and parachutist, showing a fearlessness that bordered on reckless. In addition, she was a proficient machinist and explosive expert, all skills that D. B. Cooper displayed during his hijacking.[5]

The Formans were struck with how many details about the Cooper hijacking Dayton seemed to know. She seemed to have a great deal of knowledge about how Cooper accomplished the hijacking. However, when Dayton learned that it would still be possible for her to be charged with the hijacking, she recanted her story. She died in 2002, and the FBI has never commented on her or whether she was indeed a Cooper suspect.

Other Suspects

Over the years, other people have been investigated for their connections to the Cooper case. John List, an accountant and military veteran who was convicted of murdering his wife, three children, and mother just 15 days before the NORJAK

BOOK DEAL: In 2008, the Formans wrote a book about Barbara Dayton and the Cooper connection called *The Legend of D. B. Cooper–Death by Natural Causes.*

incident, was investigated because of the timing of his crime and the fact that his appearance matched

John List might have resembled the Cooper sketches, but no direct evidence linked him to the hijacking.

many aspects of Cooper's appearance. He was captured in 1989 but never admitted to the Cooper hijacking, and the FBI dismissed him as a suspect due to lack of direct evidence.

Ted Mayfield, another military veteran and a competitive skydiver and skydiving instructor, had a criminal record and was viewed as a suspect early in the Cooper investigation. However, he was cleared, although in 2006 two amateur researchers tried to propose him as a suspect again. It was even suggested that Mayfield and the researchers had collaborated as a moneymaking scheme, although this was denied.

In 1972, a con man and ex-convict named Jack Coffelt claimed he was Cooper, hoping to sell his story to a Hollywood production company. He claimed to have landed near Mount Hood in Oregon after the hijacking, injuring himself and losing the ransom money. He did bear a resemblance to Cooper, and the FBI investigated him as a possible suspect. His story was discredited because many of the details did not match crime details known only to the FBI. Coffelt died in 1975 and his remains were cremated, so the FBI could not make a DNA comparison to Cooper.

Chapter 9

The Search Continues

Decades have passed since the NORJAK incident and the disappearance of Cooper. As time passes and those who would be Cooper's age are getting older or dying, the likelihood of apprehending Cooper or even finding out for sure who he was diminishes. As the forested areas of Washington and Oregon grow and the landscape changes, the chances of finding any hard evidence of Cooper are also reduced. And yet people continue to seek answers.

Money, Parachutes, and a Skull

There is still conjecture as to how the three bundles of money that eight-year-old Brian

Ingram found might have ended up in a sandy river bank. Officials know that in 1974, the US Army Corp of Engineers was dredging the area where the money was found, and by studying the location of the bills in relation to the sand and sediment layers, they know the bills arrived in the area after the dredging had been completed. This has led to speculation that the money floated downstream from another location or was carried by a wild animal. Others think Cooper dropped it during his descent or later buried it.

Searchers dredged the river shortly after Brian Ingram, center, found part of the ransom money.

In 1981, while searchers were looking for additional evidence along the river, a human skull was found. However, a forensic pathologist examined the skull and determined that

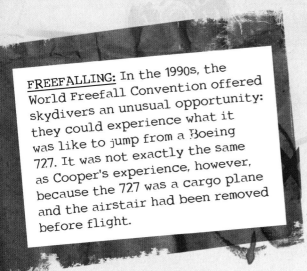

FREEFALLING: In the 1990s, the World Freefall Convention offered skydivers an unusual opportunity: they could experience what it was like to jump from a Boeing 727. It was not exactly the same as Cooper's experience, however, because the 727 was a cargo plane and the airstair had been removed before flight.

it was a woman and that she was most likely Native American.

In 1988, a small portion of a parachute was found at the bottom of the Columbia River, near the place where the money was located. However, the FBI determined it was not Copper's parachute because it was made of silk and Cooper's parachutes were made of ripstop nylon. In 2008, a group of kids found another parachute in Amboy, Washington, which is south of Lake Merwin. Again, the FBI checked it and said it could not have been Cooper's. Experts determined it was actually a vintage World War II parachute. To date, the only physical evidence of the Cooper hijacking ever found was the bundle of money and the placard from the airstair of a

The parachute discovered in 2008 was not Cooper's.

Boeing 727 airplane, which could not be positively proven to have come from the Flight 305 plane.

A Fresh Investigation

In 2007, the FBI decided to reopen the Cooper hijacking case after nearly 40 years. It felt that new techniques for investigating crimes could be used to possibly solve the only unsolved hijacking in US history. The FBI had already announced that a DNA sample had been obtained from Cooper's tie. The bureau made a deliberate effort to appeal to the public in a conversational way on its Web site:

> *Who was Cooper? Did he survive the jump? And what happened to the loot, only a small part of which has ever surfaced? It's a mystery, frankly. We've run down thousands of leads and considered all sorts of scenarios. And amateur sleuths have put forward plenty of their own theories. Yet the case remains unsolved. Would we still like to get our man? Absolutely. And we have reignited the case—thanks to a*

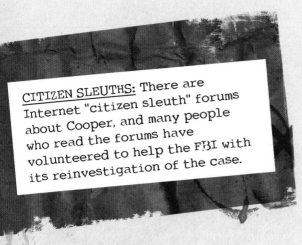

CITIZEN SLEUTHS: There are Internet "citizen sleuth" forums about Cooper, and many people who read the forums have volunteered to help the FBI with its reinvestigation of the case.

Seattle case agent named Larry Carr and new technologies like DNA testing.[1]

The FBI also released evidence and information that the public had not seen before, such as Cooper's 1971 plane ticket and the fact that one of the two reserve parachutes that had been provided to Cooper was actually a "dummy," a nonfunctioning parachute used in skydiving classrooms. Even though it was clearly marked as a training chute, Cooper selected it as the backup chute for his jump. He also chose an older primary parachute instead of a newer and better professional model. Both of these choices suggested that Cooper had not been an expert skydiver.

From Dinosaurs to Hijackers?

In the FBI's renewed request for information in the Cooper case, it had suggested that perhaps a hydrologist or other geographic expert could use modern technology to identify Cooper's landing spot. Paleontologist Tom Kaye, who usually spent his time looking for dinosaur fossils in the deserts of Wyoming, answered the challenge. He created a team that included a scientific illustrator, an expert in metals, an Egyptologist, and Brian Ingram, the same man who had found the Cooper money as a boy. They spent months investigating along the Columbia River:

> They took measurements, water and soil samples and used old FBI photographs to try to pinpoint exactly where Ingram found the money. They also placed bundles of money similar to those Cooper was given in the water to see if they floated. "No one had done that before," said [one of the team members], adding that the bundles floated for about 10 minutes.[2]

The team also used satellite maps and GPS in the hope of retracing the plane's flight path and possibly establishing exact coordinates for the place where Cooper landed. They have even used an electron microscope to study grains of pollen found on Cooper's tie, hoping that it might establish where he had been before the hijacking. Kaye did not find any evidence of pine pollen. This means that Cooper probably had not been in the Pacific Northwest before the hijacking, which has many pine trees. "After 37 years," Kaye said, "we're trying to use science to narrow all the possibilities."[3] However, the investigation did not bring any new evidence or information to light.

An Enduring Mystery

Many experts believe Cooper died skydiving from Flight 305 and that his body may lie in the bottom of the Columbia River, perhaps never to be discovered. Others believe he did survive and either died of old age or is living in hiding. Either way, the story has made Cooper into a kind of folk hero. In Ariel, Washington, near where Cooper was thought to have landed, local residents hold an annual D. B. Cooper party during which people dress up like Cooper. He seems to appeal to many people. University of Washington sociologist Otto Larsen explains how Cooper has become a kind of folk hero:

> [It was] an awesome feat in the battle of man against the machine—one man overcoming technology, the corporation, the establishment, the system. Thus, the hijacker comes off as a kind of curious Robin Hood, taking from the rich—or at least the big and complex. It doesn't matter whether he gives it to the poor.[4]

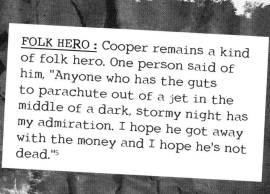

FOLK HERO : Cooper remains a kind of folk hero. One person said of him, "Anyone who has the guts to parachute out of a jet in the middle of a dark, stormy night has my admiration. I hope he got away with the money and I hope he's not dead."[5]

Himmelsbach Speaks

Many people have assumed that Himmelsbach is obsessed with the Cooper case, but he claims that he is not:

Sure, I would have liked to see the case cleaned up and to know for sure that Cooper was dead, as I believe, or to have nailed a suspect for the crime. But, that was not to be. And while I had strong feelings about wanting it closed, I was able to walk away from the case with a clear conscience that the Bureau had given the investigation the best shot. The case of D. B. Cooper has been investigated most thoroughly by the world's best investigative organization.[7]

For Himmelsbach, who probably knows more about Cooper and the hijacking than anyone else, Cooper is not a folk hero, just another criminal. He thinks there was nothing glorious or romantic about Cooper and that he most likely died alone in the wilderness with his money. "We have to accept the possibility that we may never know (any more about Cooper). I guess we can live with that, if we have to."[6]

However, in August 2011, another person came forward with information about the possible identity of Cooper. Marla Cooper contacted the FBI and said her late uncle, L. D. Cooper, may well have been D. B. Cooper. Marla had memories of seeing her uncle on the day after the hijacking took place, bloody and bruised. She remembers hearing her father and uncles talking about lost money and debating whether they should search for the cash. Marla now believes they were referring to the ransom money that was lost when Cooper leaped from the

Marla Cooper with a picture of her uncle Lynn Doyle Cooper

Dan Cooper, Comic Book Hero

The FBI thinks there may be a connection between the Cooper hijacking and a French Canadian comic book hero named Dan Cooper. The hijacker Cooper may have taken his name from the comic book series, whose hero is a Royal Canadian Air Force test pilot. One cover in the series shows Cooper parachuting. Because the comics were never published in English, they may provide a clue to the hijacker's past, if he did in fact read them and borrow the hero's name.

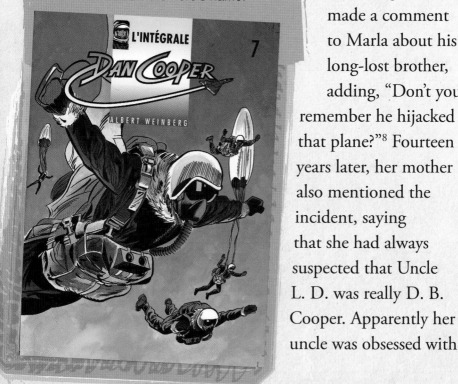

airplane and that her father said they should not search for it because the FBI was also searching the area. After that day, Marla never saw her uncle again.

Years later, when her father was dying, he made a comment to Marla about his long-lost brother, adding, "Don't you remember he hijacked that plane?"[8] Fourteen years later, her mother also mentioned the incident, saying that she had always suspected that Uncle L. D. was really D. B. Cooper. Apparently her uncle was obsessed with

94

Dan Cooper comic books, which some people believe the hijacker read. Marla eventually decided to contact the FBI, and she provided them with a photo of her uncle and his guitar

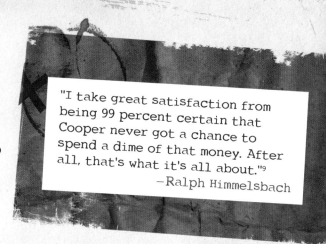

"I take great satisfaction from being 99 percent certain that Cooper never got a chance to spend a dime of that money. After all, that's what it's all about."[9]
—Ralph Himmelsbach

strap, so experts could hopefully find fingerprints or DNA evidence. The FBI is currently examining the evidence to see if there is a connection, as well as investigating a match to the DNA that was previously extracted from the tie Cooper left on the airplane. Preliminarily, FBI experts could not find fingerprints on the guitar strap to compare to fingerprints from the airplane.

D. B. Cooper's real identity and what happened to him and the rest of the ransom money may never be known. But as long as the NORJAK case is unsolved, people will keep looking for answers to the mystery.

Tools and Clues

During the Initial Investigation:

eyewitness testimony– Investigators interviewed pilots, the airline counter attendant, and flight attendants Tina Mucklow and Florence Schaffner to compile a physical description of Cooper.

fingerprints– Investigators found fingerprints on Cooper's beverage glass and in the cabin of Flight 305 but have never matched prints to a suspect.

geographic features/mapping– Investigators correlated the speed and position of Flight 305 with the geography of the land below to estimate where Cooper may have landed.

physical evidence– Cooper left his tie, tie clip, and the two remaining parachutes on the plane when he jumped.

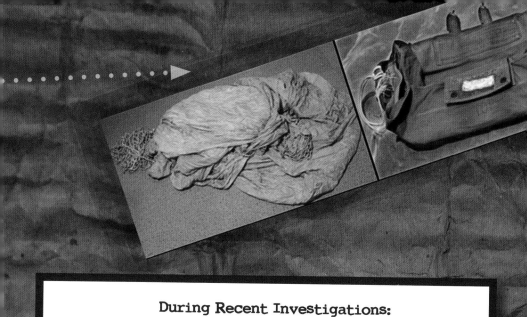

During Recent Investigations:

DNA— Investigators took DNA samples from Cooper's tie, tie clip, and glass and compared them with DNA samples from suspects.

Global Positioning System (GPS) surveying— Investigators used GPS surveying to examine the area where the Cooper ransom money was found, looking for other clues.

ransom money— Investigators used microscopes to examine the ransom money for clues about its burial.

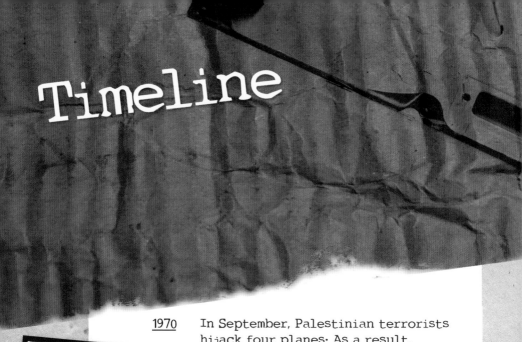

Timeline

1970   In September, Palestinian terrorists hijack four planes; As a result, President Richard Nixon mandates that sky marshals be present on certain flights.

1971   On November 24, D. B. Cooper hijacks Flight 305 on its way to the Seattle-Tacoma airport.

1971   On December 8, the serial numbers of the ransom money are released to financial institutions and shortly thereafter to the general public.

1972   The FBI conducts two large manhunts in the area where Cooper is thought to have landed in March and April.

<u>1972</u>	Richard McCoy hijacks a Boeing 727 in a manner similar to the Cooper hijacking on April 7.
<u>1972</u>	The FAA announces in December that all airlines have one month to begin searching passengers and their baggage.
<u>1974</u>	Richard McCoy is killed after escaping from prison.
<u>1977</u>	William Gossett tells a judge in Salt Lake City that he is D. B. Cooper.
<u>1980</u>	In February, Brian Ingram finds part of the Cooper ransom money in a riverbank. The FBI searches the area where the money was found.
<u>1985</u>	*D. B. Cooper: What Really Happened* is published.

Timeline

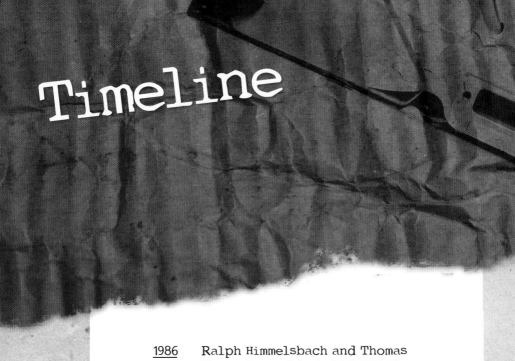

<u>1986</u>	Ralph Himmelsbach and Thomas Worcester publish *NORJAK: The Investigation of D. B. Cooper.*
<u>1991</u>	FBI agent Russell Calame publishes *D. B. Cooper: The Real McCoy,* claiming Richard McCoy was D. B. Cooper.
<u>2000</u>	An article in *US News and World Report* on July 24 states that Duane Weber confessed to being D. B. Cooper.
<u>2003</u>	Lyle Christiansen claims his brother, Kenneth, was D. B. Cooper.

2007   The FBI reopens the D. B. Cooper case.

2008   Pat and Ron Forman publish *The Legend of D. B. Cooper- Death by Natural Causes*, claiming Barbara Dayton was D. B. Cooper.

2011   Marla Cooper provides evidence to the FBI she believes implicates her uncle, L. D. Cooper.

2011   The case of D. B. Cooper and the NORJAK incident remains open.

Glossary

airspeed . . . . The measure of how fast an airplane is traveling through the air.

airstair . . . . The rear fold-down stairs located under the tail section of an airplane.

civilian . . . . A person who is not an active member of the military.

courier . . . . A messenger, usually one carrying urgent or important news.

deploy . . . . To move into position for use.

dredging . . . . Scraping mud, sand, and rocks from the bottom of a river, lake, or other body of water.

extortion . . . . To get money or information using violence, threats, or abuse of authority.

indict. . . . . To bring a formal accusation against someone; to charge with a crime.

microfilm. . . . . A type of film on which printed materials are photographed and saved, to make storage easier.

paratrooper . . . . A soldier who is trained to use a parachute, especially in battle situations.

placard . . . . A sign or notice, usually made from heavy paper, poster board, or plastic.

purser . . . . A flight attendant who works with customs and immigration officials and manages the plane's money.

serial number. . . . . . A specific number that is used to identify something such as currency, vehicles, or equipment.

terrain. . . . . The natural features of a portion of land.

terrorist. . . . . A person who uses violence to threaten people or a government.

Additional Resources

Selected Bibliography

"D. B. Cooper Redux: Help Us Solve an Enduring Mystery." *The Federal Bureau of Investigation*. FBI.gov, 31 Dec. 2007. Web. 16 Aug. 2011.

Gray, Geoffrey. "Unmasking D. B. Cooper." *New York Magazine*. New York Media, 21 Oct. 2007. Web. 16 Aug. 2011.

Himmelsbach, Ralph P., and Thomas K. Worcester. *NORJAK: The Investigation of D. B. Cooper*. West Linn, OR: Norjak Project, 1986. Print.

Porteous, Skipp, and Robert Blevins. *Into the Blast: The True Story of D. B. Cooper*. Revised edition. Seattle, WA: Adventure Books, 2011. Print.

Further Readings

Karlitz, Gail. *Virtual Apprentice: FBI Agent*. New York: Ferguson, 2009. Print.

Schroeder, Andreas. *Thieves! True Stories from the Edge*. Toronto: Annick, 2005. Print.

Web Links

To learn more about the D. B. Cooper hijacking, visit ABDO Publishing Company online at **www.abdopublishing.com**. Web sites about the D. B. Cooper hijacking are featured on our Book Links page. These links are routinely monitored and updated to provide the most current information available.

Places to Visit

FBI Headquarters
National Museum of Crime and Punishment
575 Seventh Street NW, Washington, DC 20004
202-621-5550
http://www.crimemuseum.org
This museum features exhibits on crime scene investigation
techniques and crime history and driving and shooting simulators
that give visitors a feel for police work.

Museum of Science and Industry
Fifty-Seventh Street and Lake Shore Drive, Chicago, IL 60637
773-684-1414
http://www.msichicago.org
This museum has an actual Boeing 727 on exhibit, the same kind
of plane used in the Cooper hijacking.

Newseum
555 Pennsylvania Avenue NW, Washington, DC 20001
888-639-7386
http://www.newseum.org
A museum on the history of news reporting, with exhibits and
hands-on activities.

Source Notes

Chapter 1. Hijack!

1. "D. B. Cooper Redux: Help Us Solve an Enduring Mystery." *The Federal Bureau of Investigation*. FBI.gov, 31 Dec. 2007. Web. 16 Aug. 2011.

2. Ben Welter. "The D. B. Cooper Hijacking." *Minneapolis Star Tribune*. Star Tribune, 29 Oct. 2007. Web. 16 Aug. 2011.

3. Ibid.

4. Ibid.

5. Ibid.

6. Ibid.

7. Ibid.

Chapter 2. An Era of Trust

1. "The Samurai Airplane Hijackers." *Newspaper Archive*. Heritage Microfilm, 2009. Web. 16 Aug. 2011.

2. Annie Wu. "History of Airport Security." *The Savvy Traveler*. American Public Media, n.d. Web. 16 Aug. 2011.

3. Ibid.

4. Ibid.

Chapter 3. Flight 305

1. Richard Seven. "D. B. Cooper—Perfect Crime or Perfect Folly?" *Seattle Times*. Seattle Times, 17 Nov. 1996. Web. 16 Aug. 2011.

2. Scott Schwebke, "D. B. Cooper mystery—Did Witness See Hijacker's Parachute?" Ogden *Standard-Examiner*. Standard-Examiner, May 23, 2010. Web. 16 Aug. 2011.

Chapter 4. The Hunt Is On

1. "Codename: Norjak: The Skyjacking of Northwest Flight 305." *Check-Six.com*. Check-Six.com, n.d. Web. 16 Aug. 2011.

2. Ibid.

3. "D. B. Cooper Redux: Help Us Solve an Enduring Mystery." *The Federal Bureau of Investigation*. FBI.gov, 31 Dec. 2007. Web. 16 Aug. 2011.

4. Richard Seven. "D. B. Cooper—Perfect Crime or Perfect Folly?" *Seattle Times*. Seattle Times, 17 Nov. 1996. Web. 16 Aug. 2011.

Chapter 5. A Copycat Crime . . . or Cooper?

1. "Famous Cases and Criminals: Richard Floyd McCoy, Jr.—Aircraft Hijacking." *The Federal Bureau of Investigation*. FBI.gov, n.d. Web. 16 Aug. 2011.

2. Ibid.

3. Musika Farnsworth. "Skyjacker: The Richard McCoy Story, Part 2," *Parachutist*. United States Parachute Association, 13 Apr. 2011. Web. 16 Aug. 2011.

4. "Famous Cases and Criminals: Richard Floyd McCoy, Jr.—Aircraft Hijacking." *The Federal Bureau of Investigation*. FBI.gov, n.d. Web. 16 Aug. 2011.

5. David Krajicek. "D. B. Cooper: The Legendary Daredevil—Copycats." *TruTV Crime Library*. Turner Entertainment, n.d. Web. 16 Aug. 2011.

6. Ibid.

Chapter 6. Confessions

1. Douglas Pasternak. "Skyjacker at Large." *US News Online*. US News and World Report, 24 July 2000. Web. 16 Aug. 2011.

2. Ibid.

3. Ibid.

4. Warwick Sabin and Max Brantley. "Mena Man to Sell D. B. Cooper Cash." *Arkansas Times*. Arkansas Times, 26 Jan. 2006. Web. 16 Aug. 2011.

5. Ralph P. Himmelsbach and Thomas K. Worcester. *NORJAK: The Investigation of D. B. Cooper.* West Linn, OR: Norjak Project, 1986. Print. 109.

6. Warwick Sabin and Max Brantley. "Mena Man to Sell D. B. Cooper Cash." *Arkansas Times.* Arkansas Times, 26 Jan. 2006. Web. 16 Aug. 2011.

7. "PCGS Currency Notifies FBI of 'D. B. Cooper' Serial Numbers." *Professional Coin Grading Service.* Collectors Universe, 27 Feb. 2008. Web. 16 Aug. 2011.

8. Ralph P. Himmelsbach and Thomas K. Worcester. *NORJAK: The Investigation of D. B. Cooper.* West Linn, OR: Norjak Project, 1986. Print. 132.

Chapter 7. A Dead Ringer

1. Geoffrey Gray. "Unmasking D. B. Cooper." *New York Magazine.* New York Media, 21 Oct. 2007. Web. 16 Aug. 2011.

2. Ibid.

3. Ibid.

4. Ibid.

5. Ibid.

6. Ibid.

7. Ibid.

Chapter 8. A Son's Suspicions

1. "Did D. B. Cooper Retire to Oregon Coast?" *KATU.com.* KATU News, 20 Nov. 2008. Web. 16 Aug. 2011.

2. John S. Craig. "D. B. Cooper Suspect Named: William Pratt Gossett." *Associated Content.* Yahoo, June 2011. Web. 16 Aug. 2011.

3. Ibid.

4. Ibid.

5. Bruce A. Smith. "Local Authors Pen Dramatic Story about Skyjacking Legend D. B. Cooper." *Eatonville Dispatch*. Dispatch, 22 Aug. 2008. Web. 16 Aug. 2011.

Chapter 9. The Search Continues

1. "D. B. Cooper Redux: Help Us Solve an Enduring Mystery." *The Federal Bureau of Investigation*. FBI.gov, 31 Dec. 2007. Web. 16 Aug. 2011.

2. Les Blumenthal. "Citizen Sleuths Follow Trail of Elusive Hijacker D. B. Cooper." *McClatchy*. McClatchy, 20 Apr. 2009. Web. 16 Aug. 2011.

3. Jeff Darnell. "Legend of D. B. Cooper." *National Geographic Blog*. National Geography Society, 26 July 2009. Web. 16 Aug. 2011.

4. "D. B. Cooper: A Crime Immortalized by Time." *The Columbian*. Columbian, n.d. web. 16 Aug. 2011.

5. Ralph P. Himmelsbach and Thomas K. Worcester. *NORJAK: The Investigation of D. B. Cooper*. West Linn, OR: Norjak Project, 1986. Print. 116.

6. "D. B. Cooper: A Crime Immortalized by Time." *The Columbian*. Columbian, n.d. web. 16 Aug. 2011.

7. Ralph P. Himmelsbach and Thomas K. Worcester. *NORJAK: The Investigation of D. B. Cooper*. West Linn, OR: Norjak Project, 1986. Print. 122.

8. Pierre Thomas and Jack Cloherty. "D. B. Cooper Exclusive: Did Niece Provide Key Evidence?" *ABC News*. ABC News, 3 Aug. 2011. Web. 16 Aug. 2011.

9. Ralph P. Himmelsbach and Thomas K. Worcester. *NORJAK: The Investigation of D. B. Cooper*. West Linn, OR: Norjak Project, 1986. Print. 129.

Index

About the Author

Marcia Amidon Lusted has written more than 60 books for young readers, as well as hundreds of magazine articles. She is an assistant editor for Cobblestone Publishing, a writing instructor, and a musician. She lives in New Hampshire.

About the Content Consultant

Michael Stapleton retired from the Federal Bureau of Investigation following a 34-year career. His investigations included the D. B. Cooper hijacking, the Oklahoma City Federal Building bombing, and the Unabomber case. He is the founder of Forensics R Us and Stapleton & Associates, LLC, both forensics consulting firms. He holds a master's degree in Instructional Technology from San Jose State University and is an adjunct professor with the American River College, Sacramento Regional Public Safety Training Center, in Sacramento, California.

Photo Credits

AP Images, cover, 3, 11, 15, 27, 31, 38, 63, 67 (left), 82, 96 (bottom), 98 (top), 98 (bottom), 100 (left), 105; CSU Archives/Everett Collection Inc/ Alamy, 7; Popperfoto/Getty Images, 17; Harold Valentine/AP Images, 19; Joe Demaria/AP Images, 23; Ken Tannenbaum/Shutterstock Images, 25; Federal Bureau of Investigation, 29, 97 (top); Co Rentmeester/Time & Life Pictures/Getty Images, 32; Melanie Conner, 35; Red Line Editorial, 37, 58, 96 (top); Mark Stephan/Bigstock, 40; Edward Kitch/AP Images, 45; Daniel Hurst/Bigstock, 46; Wally Fong/AP Images, 50; Eric Risberg/ AP Images, 59, 97 (bottom); Wes Guderian/The Oregonian, 61; Sherlock Investigations, 67 (right), 100 (right); Universal Pictures/Photofest, 68; U.S. Army Signal Corps/AP Images, 70; David Falconer/The Oregonian, 79; Rob Crandall/AP Images, 85, 99; Kevin P. Casey/AP Images, 87; Sue Ogrocki/AP Images, 93, 101; MCT/Getty Images, 94